The Mermaid and the Cow

By Lindsey Cole

There once lived a mermaid in a beautiful river.

She swam with the animals and sang with the birds.

It really was a very happy river.

This book belongs to...

....

For all the mini eco warriors out there.
And for Sam, the poorly cat, who visited me for the last
three weeks of his life and helped me finish this book.

ISBN: 978-1-8382665-0-9
Printed and bound in Wales by Gomer Press, Llandysul

People also liked to use the river.
But they began to leave a lot of mess.

One day, a fierce storm raged through the countryside and blew the rubbish **EVERYWHERE.**

The mermaid watched sadly as the plastic put the animals in terrible danger.

It got tangled in the reeds and trees and floated on the river like a noodle soup. Some animals mistook it for food.

It was not a happy river anymore.

The mermaid tried her hardest to pick up all the rubbish. But the more she reached for, the more it slipped from her grip.

Some of the plastic was really sharp, and it cut the mermaid's hand.

Despite all her hard work, the plastic **NEVER** went away.

The mermaid realised there was far too much rubbish for her to clean on her own, so she decided to swim downstream to look for help.

On the bank, she spotted a fisherman and his son.

"Hello, could you possibly help me?" the mermaid began.

But the fisherman didn't want to be disturbed.

Next, she saw a dog walker.
But she was too busy talking on her phone.

And the family picnicking were having too much fun to even notice her.

The mermaid swam on until she came across the biggest plastic bag she'd ever seen, tangled in a tree.

OowOoooooooo!

"It's hopeless," she wailed. "No one wants to help me clean the river. It will always be a horrible mess."

As she tugged at the bag a noise came from behind the tree.

It wasn't a big plastic bag at all - it was a...

... cow!

"What are you doing in the water?" The mermaid gasped.

"I slipped in when I was reaching for my favourite juicy grass by the river bank. Now my calf will be lost, wondering where I am," the cow sobbed.

"You poor cow," the mermaid replied. She really wanted to help - but cows are **REALLY** heavy.

They're heavier than twenty bathing mermaids.

And they are certainly heavier than a squillion sloppy **COW PATS!**

They're heavier than 100,000 slimy frogs.

"I'm going to be stuck here **FOREVER!**"
The cow cried.

The mermaid looked at a bird that landed on the
cow's head and thought quietly for a while. Then
she smiled and said, "No you won't. I have an idea!"

She climbed up onto a rock and started to sing...

"Dear darling birds and wildlife friends,
I need your help on this river bend.
Please bring to me that plastic so tough,
To help get our friend here out of the rough."

Her beautiful song filled the air and carried her words down the winding river.

Before long, birds and animals started to appear, all clutching bits of plastic just as the mermaid had asked.

"Let's turn all this rubbish into something useful, to help get the cow out of the river," the mermaid said.

The birds swooshed into a colossal murmuration, and spun the plastic into an enormous piece of extra strong rope.

Then, they swooped down and gave the rope to the animals who looped it around the cow.

MOOOOOOOO!

As the birds flapped their wings and tugged the upcycled rope the mermaid pushed the cow's bottom as hard as she could.

The cow shot out of the river and flew so high into the sky that her calf spotted her from the distant hills.

The cow was so happy to be out of the river and reunited with her calf, she gave the mermaid a big lick and said, "How can I ever thank you?"

The mermaid smiled as she saw a news reporter heading towards them. "I think you've already done plenty. This is just what we need to let everyone know about the plastics problem!"

The following day, the mermaid's cow rescue was all over the news...

Everyone turned up to help the mermaid clear the rubbish, and restore her home to a beautiful, happy river once more.

The cow and her calf trotted along the bank making sure no one dropped litter ever again.

So, the next time you see a cow beside a river, there might just be a mermaid nearby too. And always remember to...

Can you help save the mermaids and their friends?

We need to act **now**, if we want to help the mermaids and their friends. When Lindsey's not a mermaid she calls herself an **Urban Mermaid**. You can be one too!

- Use reusable bags, bottles, pots and cups, so you can refuse single use plastic. There's fun looking ones out there or you could even decorate yours, perhaps with a mermaid and a cow?

- Pick up rubbish anywhere you go. Give yourself a big sloppy cow pat on the back if you pick up more pieces than you did last time. Keep a chart to see how well you're doing.

- Reduce the amount of rubbish in your household. Collect all the rubbish that you do use, and turn it into a mermaid mural to remind yourself what items to avoid next time.

- Give your old belongings a new purpose, before chucking them in the bin. Lindsey turned friends' old swimsuits into a fabulous new mermaid tail. See what you can create!

Keep Lindsey posted! Take a photo and tag **@stompycole** and **#urbanmermaidclub** to let her know how you get on. For more fun activities and workshops join the Urban Mermaid club at **www.lindseycole.co.uk/urban-mermaid**

Proceeds from this book go towards helping *We Swim Wild* fund essential microplastic research across Britain.

About the author

After cutting her hand on a piece of plastic while free diving in Indonesia Lindsey wanted to do something about plastic pollution. So she swam 120 miles of the River Thames in a mermaid tail to highlight how we're choking our wildlife with plastic. With artist Barbara de Moubray as canoe support, they towed a mermaid sculpture made from recycled plastic, stuffing it with all the waste they found. Along the way they found a cow stranded in the river and called the RSPCA. Six firemen wrapped their hose around the cow to haul her out. After spending a night at the vet's, the cow was reunited with her calf the following day- and Mermaid Saves Drowning Cow was the headline on page three of a national tabloid!

Lindsey visits schools to share her story and runs environmental workshops. With her new sustainably-made mermaid tail, Lindsey has more swimming adventures planned, together with a series of children's books.

To keep up to date with Lindsey's mermaid swims and other adventures, please visit
www.lindseycole.co.uk

The Mermaid and the Cow was funded directly by readers. The names listed below are of kind supporters who pledged to make this book happen and made Lindsey udderly grateful.

Mya & Thea Henderson • Rowan Clarke • Sue Barrett • Mia & Max Pluckrose • Sarah Williams • Emma & Arthur Harper • Katharine Ferguson • Christine Cole • Rebekah Taylor • Maggie Thorpe-Kerr • Laura & Mabon Sanderson • Andrew Judge • Chloe & Sophie Jalland • Cheryl Harvey • Amy Baker • Lulu Stephen • Victoria Gaunt • Laura Humphries • Anne-Laure Carruth • Laura Watts • Fiona Hunter • Victoria Dacey • Nina Saada • James Fuller • Isabel Sinagola • Zoe Dunford • Nikki Swinbrun • Kate Olson • Bethan Palmer • Annie Thomas • Colin Campbell • Tim Webb • Mary Moykan • Fiona Guest • Andy Howlett • Des Pellicena • Siobhan E James • Ian, Jo & Cora Straker • Debbie Travers • Scott Dawson • Catherine Hoy • Tim Osborn-Jones • Menna Wakeford • Karen Smith • Ruth Roberts • Scarlett & Oscar Liddle • Stuart Harrison • Stephen Mackay • Dom Edwards • Hollie Thomson • Calum Maclean • Jaimi Wilson • The Reddicks • Helen Turner • Kasia Fiderkiewicz • Rebecca Caplan • Amelia Stewart • Sonia Michaelsen • Fi Redpath • Flo and Nell Dew • Natalie Pilgrim • Julia Snaith • Gwenllian Hughes • Daisy Skelley • Ramin Jarvand • Tommo Stuart • Peter Salmon • Cecile Burton • Alex Wilson • Lou Jones • Rebecca Lidster-Lyons • Beth Waddington-Smith • Moira Gunn • Anushka Chakravarty • Amy Wilson • Ameera Fletcher • Mary Rai • Oli Hunter-Smart • George Thomas • Andy & Olive Smith • Jo Geneen • Cory Hughes • Sally Low • Miranda Sharp • Rosie Cripps • Amy Golding • Chris Lyddiatt • Mike Brook • James Dillon • Lu Watkins • Joanna Gordon • Wendy Ives • Karin Robinson • Antonia Chappele • Parliament Hill Lido • Joanna Nightongale • Lucy Barnes • Olivia Bowles • Samantha Crowe • Kate, Sophie & Eddy Mayhew • Ella Foote • Katrina Dainton • Laura Kavanagh • Charlotte Wilsher • Clare Khaghani • Bridget Gronow • Jessica Dearden-Hall • Mary Stokes • Chantal Cunningham • Cameron Hall • Tom Dudden • Bea & Rory • Tim Clouter • Emma Hipkiss • Nick Woodrow • Jo Tennant • Keri Hutchinson • Caroline McShane • Bruce Mayhew • Mark Ostheimer • Katie Marston • Leon Fryer • Jennie Sallis • Lucie Muddell • Mariota Dunning • Ranulph & Darcie Ball • Vicki Egarr • Gethin & Maurice Mullin • Lisa Lloyd • Corinne Heggie • Omie-Elizabeth Dale • Richard Craddock • Jocelyn Sanford • Rowena Chiu • Katie Hamilton • Kathryn de Ferrer • Rebecca Weeks • J Bryan • Frances Dartford • Bobbie Barron • Barge East • Karen Biles • Andy Parritt